For my little Else.
A kiss from your giant - CN

Text copyright © 2004 Carl Norac
Illustrations copyright © 2004 Ingrid Godon
Moral rights asserted
Dual language copyright © 2004 Mantra Lingua
All rights reserved
A CIP record for this book is available from the British Library
First published in 2004 by Macmillan Children's Books, London
First dual language publication in 2004 by Mantra Lingua
This edition 2012

Global House, 303 Ballards Lane,
London N12 8NP
www.mantralingua.com

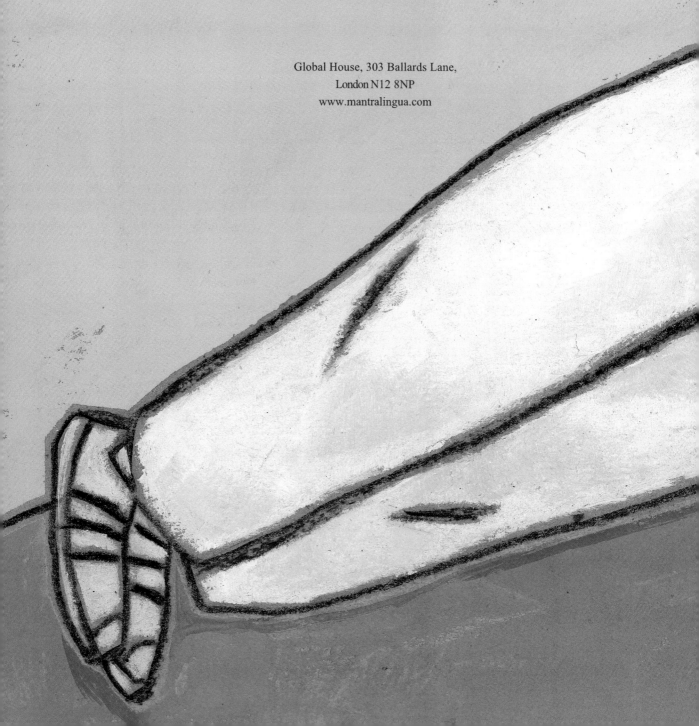

CARL NORAC
INGRID GODON

Moj je tatek div
My Daddy is a Giant

Croatian translation by Dubravka Janekovic

mantra

Moj je tatek div.
Kada se poželim s njima pomaziti,
Moram se popeti na ljestve.

My daddy is a giant.
When I want to cuddle him,
I have to climb a ladder.

Kada se igramo skrivača
tata se mora sakriti
iza brijega.

When we play hide-and-seek,
my daddy has to hide
behind a mountain.

A kada se oblaci umore,
onda dođu do mog tateka
i spavaju mu na ramenima.

And when the clouds are tired,
they come and sleep
on my daddy's shoulders.

Kada tata kihne,
more uzburka tako,
kao kada puše bura iz sve snage.

When my daddy sneezes,
it's like a hurricane.
It blows the sea away.

Kad se tatek smije
to je kao neka druga bura.
S grana svo lišće pada na sve strane.

When my daddy laughs,
it's like another hurricane.
All the leaves fly off the trees.

Ptičice vole moga taticu
pa se gnijezde u njegovoj kosi.

Birds love my daddy.
They make their nests
in his hair.

Kada igramo nogomet
tata uvijek pobjeđuje.
Od njegova udarca lopta može
odletjeti čak do mjeseca.

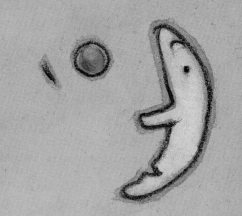

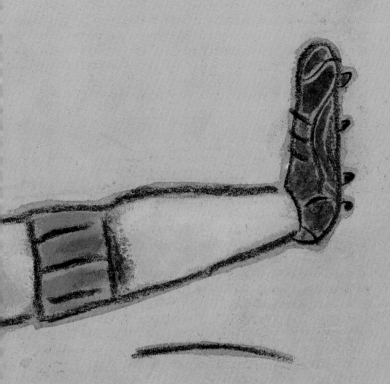

When we play football,
my daddy always wins.

He can kick the ball as high as the moon.

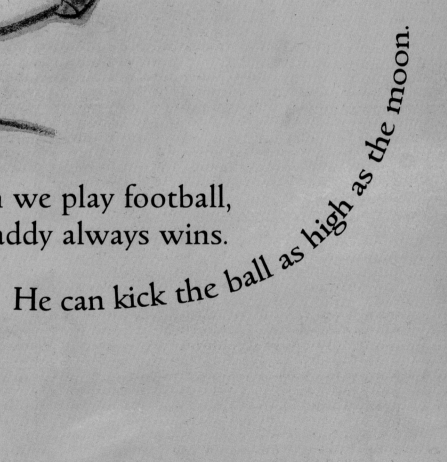

Ali ja uvijek pobjeđujem kada se pikulamo.
Njegovi su prsti preveliki.

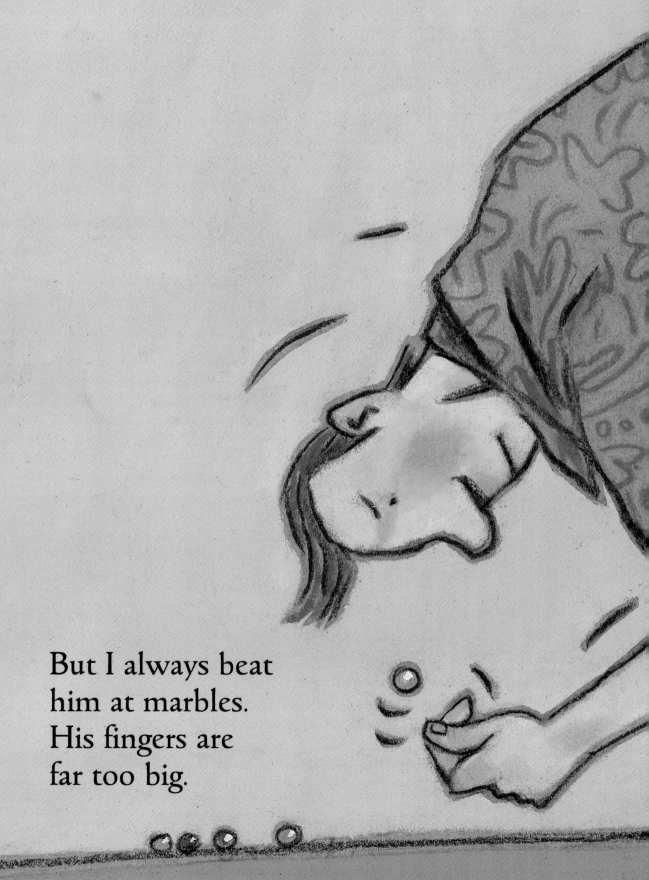

But I always beat
him at marbles.
His fingers are
far too big.

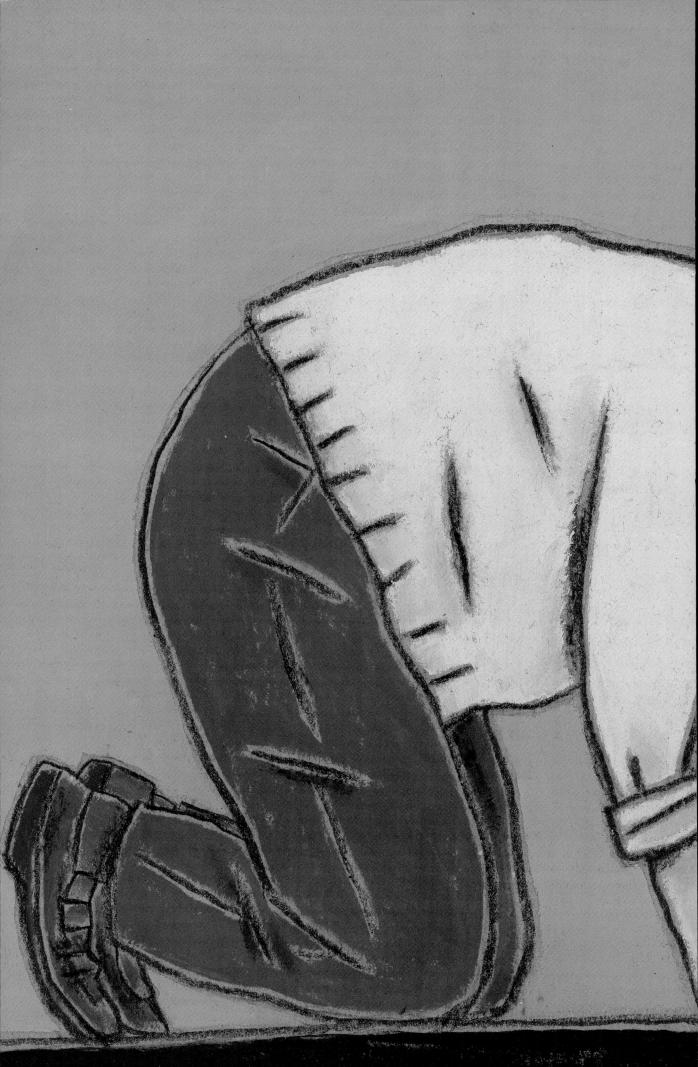

Volim kada tata kaže,
"Uskoro ćeš biti visok k'o ja!"

I like it when my
daddy says,
"You're getting as
tall as me!"

Kada moj tata trči
zemlja se trese
kao da je muči silan strah.

When my daddy runs,

the ground shakes

as if it was scared.

Ali ja se ne bojim ničega
kada me drži
moj tata na svojim rukama.

But I'm not scared
of anything when
I'm in my daddy's arms.

Moj je otac div
i on me voli od sveg
svog divovskog srca.

My daddy is a giant,
and he loves me with
all his giant heart.

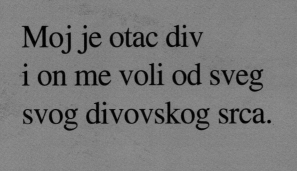